This is NOT a "cook book"!

It's not designed to teach you how to cook, or to provide complete instructions.

... but if you need more detail, there are lots of recipes online!

These are drawings to help you remember easy, tasty things to eat!

Yum!

Don't Forget to Eat!
Published by jammyness.com
PO Box 19516 New West Station PO, New Westminster BC V3M1B0, Canada
Printed in the United States by Lulu Press, Inc
Don't Forget to Eat © jam 2020 . All rights reserved.
ISBN 978-0-9866591-6-4

When I'm feeling over- whelmed or sad, I often forget how to turn ingredients into meals.

...but even a small reminder can get me thru a basic meal.

(all food is good food♡)

Healthy food is vital to get you through tough times!

FALL WINTER SPRING SUMMER

organized by season!

Use these zines as inspiration!

You deserve healthy, delicious food!

♡Jam!
2020

SPRING

CUCUMBER

SANDWICH!

✧ easy and ✧
✧ refreshing! ✧

mayo

salt & pepper

cream cheese & dill or chives or ranch dressing.

Quiche!

sautéed onion

tomatoes

pepper

mushrooms

spinach

asparagus

cheese

frozen pie crust
pre-bake per instructions

3 eggs + 1/2 c milk

S & P

bake @ 350F

30-45m

Spinach Salad

egg

smoked tofu

goat cheese

cucumber

fruit

nuts, seeds, craisins

radishes

oil, balsamic vinegar, salt & pepper

oil & cider vinegar + garlic & red pepper flakes

oil & cider vinegar + honey & mustard

pad thai

tofu

egg

lime

red pepper

rice noodles

peanuts

cilantro &/o spring onion

bean sprouts

— SAUCE —

2 tbs
soy sauce

2 tbs
mushroom sauce

1 tsp
sugar

grill cheese

tomato

egg!

try sourdough!

basil

mustard &/or mayo

red pepper flakes

Stir Fry!

sesame seeds

broccoli

peas

mushrooms

onion

carrots

peppers

tofu

soy sauce

sesame oil

brown sugar

sriracha

mush. sauce

tomato egg

1. beat egg & chop tomato
   salt
   or can of diced

2. pre-cook eggs halfway

3. cook down tomatoes
   eggs aside
   sugar
   sugar
   s&p

4. cook all together!
   eggs

yogurt!

it's good!

banana!

cimamon

MIX
&MATCH

lemon

berries

seeds
or nuts

granola

chocolate
chips

honey

jam

Summer

Cubed Watermelon

Sometimes you can get it pre-chopped!

✦ Taco Bowl! ✦

Rice (base)

BEANS
(black or
garbanzo)

AVOCADO

CORN

SALSA &
TOMATO

YAM or
SWEET POTATO

LIME +
CILANTRO

SOUR
CREAM

+ cheddar cheese!
+ beef

Avocado Toast

butter

avocado

salt + pepper

PASTA SALAD

rotini
cooked &
cooled

yogurt, mayo
or oil & vinegar

chickpeas

peas

dill or
cilantro

cheese
or
smoked
tofu

red
onion

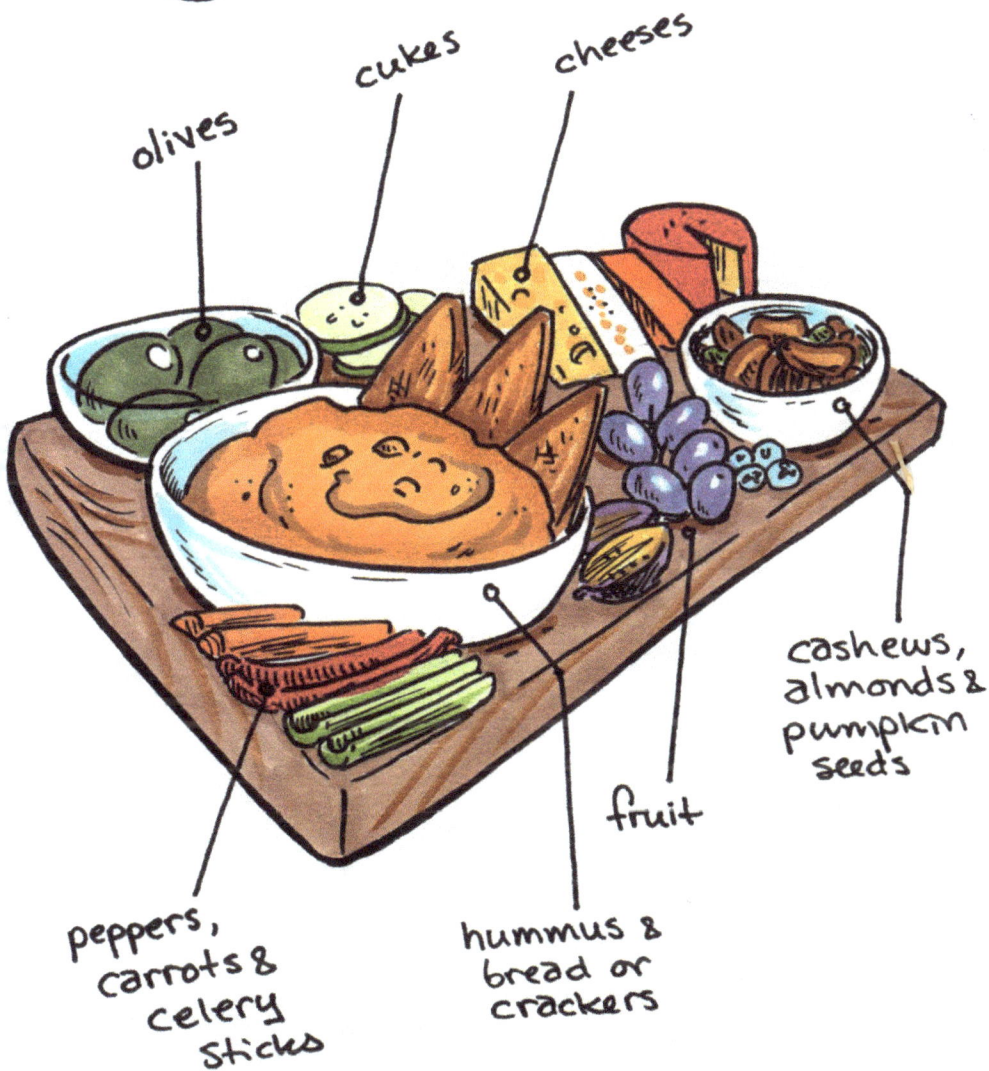

Charcuterie

olives

cukes

cheeses

cashews, almonds & pumpkin seeds

fruit

peppers, carrots & celery sticks

hummus & bread or crackers

FALL

harvest bowl

pumpkin seeds

spinach or kale

sweet potato

roasted chickpeas or black beans

mushrooms

tofu

tahini + lemon + oil + salt

brown rice

lime

zucchini

cilantro

pomegranate seeds or craisins

roast or steam in instant pot

or squash

baked potato!

salsa & corn **or** chili **or** cheese, chives & sour cream **or** caramelized onions & mushrooms **or** brocoli & cheese **or** peas & curry **or** egg...

BASICS!

butter

S P

don't forget to pierce with a fork

Ø no foil!

foil + oven
400°F/1h

instant pot
1c water/14m

microwave
7-10m

quesadilla!

black beans

sautéed mushrooms

tomato slices or salsa

just toast & flip!

sour cream

salsa

2 tortillas, cheese & fillings

dumplings!

sesame oil
chili oil
garlic
soy sauce
rice vinegar

boil

pan fry

bake

CHILI!

① oil, pepper, onion, 4 garlic cloves → sauté

② 2 cans beans (Kidney, garbanzo, black or pinto, or mix!)

28oz diced tomatoes

to cover — veg broth, or...

20-30m simmer — 30m natural release

③

1T chili pow, 2tsp oregano, 1tsp cumin

S & P

optional: celery, corn, carrot, mushrooms, bay leaf, liquid smoke

Ravioli

w/ bonus egg!

also try:
- sautéed mushrooms
- spinach

①
Store bought ravioli is FAST & freezes well!

②
Boil!

w/ a bit of extra time, you can make sauce from scratch

③
pasta sauce

④ ≈ extras! ≈

basil

cheese

tomato rice

tofu

sesame seeds

steamed bok choi

Kimchi

mushrooms

some veg can be cooked right in the rice pot, too!

- mushrooms
- squash
- brocobli

place ½ tomato face-down in a rice cooker with rice & lentils

Oil S P

when done, mash the tomato up in the rice

fall fruits

in salads

in oatmeal

sliced & raw

in crumbles

in muffins & pies & pancakes

WINTER

split pea
SOUP!

Risotto

try:
- mushroom
- squash or pumpkin
- asparagus & lemon
- tomato

onion & garlic

sautée in 2 tbsp butter +1 tbsp oil

2c raw rice

sautée raw rice until translucent

4c stock   3/4c white wine or apple cider vinegar

optional: miso paste

cook while stirring until liquid absorbs (or instant pot 7m)

Shepherd's* pie

mashed ♡ potatoes

corn

peas & carrots

veg filling:
- Lentils &/or
- mushrooms &/or
- veg "meat" Substitute

* or "cottage pie"
idk w/e

shakshuka

 sautée
pepper
onion
garlic
+ tomato paste

 add & cook tomatos
 diced

salt, pepper & paprika

 drop in eggs

cover pan & cook until eggs are done
 shh

top with feta

 cilantro or parsley or green onion

CURRY!

japanese ~gravy~ daht~ **indian** coconut ~tomato~ ~shrimp~ **thai**

meat + potatoes **Style** chick peas **Style** chicken **Style** ~red ~green ~yellow

ready-made pastes & cubes

glico

try:

chickpeas

tofu

squash

onion

peas

carrot

potatoes

Mac & Cheese!

Try:

Cauliflower instead of pasta!

butternut squash (instead of some cheese)

panko bread crumb topping

bibimbap!

☆ use what you've got! ☆

"greens"
- bok choi
- sliced cucumber
- sautéed spinach
- zucchini

+ "reds"
- KIMCHi
- mushrooms
- shredded carrot
- radishes

+ "whites"
- bean sprouts
- tofu
- shredded cabbage

nori sheets

sesame seeds

+ egg on top

bed of rice

+ sauce = hot pepper paste 2 tbsp

GOCHUJANG

+ soy sauce 1 tbsp
sesame oil 1 tbsp
rice vinegar 1 tsp
water 1 tbsp

+

1 tbsp brown sugar

1 tsp garlic (minced)

Oranges!

- easy snack or dessert
- add to salads
- use as glaze/sauce

Thanks to the patrons who made this zine possible!

Miles♥Aldous Russell♥Anna Walsh♥Sean Horn♥RJAR ♥Lisa ♥Christopher Chung
♥Yurgan Urjack♥HardZero ♥Damon Hart-Davis♥Wolfgang Behrens♥Capucine ♥Dylan
♥Stacy Nicole♥Probably Human♥Kai ♥Phill Peach♥Thomas Pritchard♥Ada Kerman
♥Boreas ♥kelly bush♥Anna Izenman♥Daniel DeRosia♥Amy Poli♥Wayne Dang
♥Andrew Swanton♥Tina Nichols♥Ilana ♥Tina Klassen♥Raphael ♥Amelia Meyer
♥Blake Rothwell♥Melissa Nurmi♥Ewe Knee Knot Know♥K Fung♥Glade
♥Patrick Bernier ♥Caleb Amos♥Christine ♥Matt Zweig♥Matthew Powell
♥Christopher Schurman♥Sune Ewert Astrup♥Christopher♥Tanya ♥Melissa Huston
♥Joanna ♥Henrik Lindhe♥Fárbás Tamás♥Kevin ♥Anthony Gilberti♥Mike Purvis
♥Patrick Naish♥Erik Edberg♥Holly B♥Patrick Hallal♥Ilearch n'n'daCorna♥Elaine Short
♥Maddy B♥Amos Onn♥Tim Willmott♥Amanda Chou♥Dean Bailey♥kaitou
♥Jed Spradling♥Lewis Allen♥Giles Sutcliffe♥Svend Andersen♥William Hector
♥Lauren Singer♥Scott ♥Daniel Karnes♥Bria Morgan♥Billy ♥Brandon Kirisaki
♥Kris Lipscombe♥Jamie Furtner♥Jeph Jacques♥Peter Kempson♥Joe ♥Jens Banning
♥Stefan Schmiedl♥Justin Sorbello♥Daniel Cornelius♥pikafoop ♥IcyMidnight
♥Alexander Botkin♥Charlie Owen♥Ali ♥David Drum♥Juan Chanco♥Christopher Ingram
♥Brian Kim♥Kathleen Ralph♥Sinogen ♥Cindy Norton♥James A. Thornton♥Karl Dahlberg
♥Becky Landry♥Phil ♥Faith Nelson♥NJGR ♥Mattis Jensen♥Chris Russell♥calicosarah
♥Bryce Chidester♥Delta-Fox ♥Doctor Professor♥Parabet♥Ricardo Bittencourt♥Jeff Grafton
♥BearPerson ♥Dave Coleman♥Logan Arias♥   July 2020

www.ingramcontent.com/pod-product-compliance
Lightning Source LLC
Chambersburg PA
CBHW041535070426
42452CB00046B/2967